Contents

Ready to go

Strapped in and ready to go, you stare through the windscreen of your highly specialized car. The road before you leads to the stunt you've been waiting to pull off. The engine idles. Your body tingles with excitement and fear. The stunt has been researched and approved for safety. But there is still an element of danger.

You ease the car forwards gently and take a deep breath. As you pick up speed, you hit the accelerator and give it all the car has to give. You approach a ramp, and then you launch. In mid-air everything is quiet. You're flying! You soar over flaming boxes, or other cars, or water. You land with a jolt and slow down. As quickly as it starts, it's over. You've done it! You are an incredible stunt driver.

Car and driver pull off a fiery stunt at the
Prometheus Festival of Stunt Art in Moscow, Russia

Pushing the limits

The car comes to life

In 1886, German Karl Benz patented the first gasoline-powered automobile. It was a mechanical marvel that could move people and cargo from place to place without using horses. However, it was quite slow and difficult to *manoeuvre* with just three wheels. Within five years Benz upgraded his design to make a four-wheeled car that greatly improved the machine's stability. As cars became more powerful, faster and safer, the limits to what they could do also expanded.

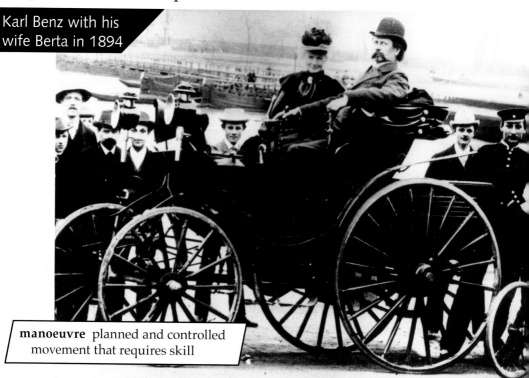

Karl Benz with his wife Berta in 1894

manoeuvre planned and controlled movement that requires skill

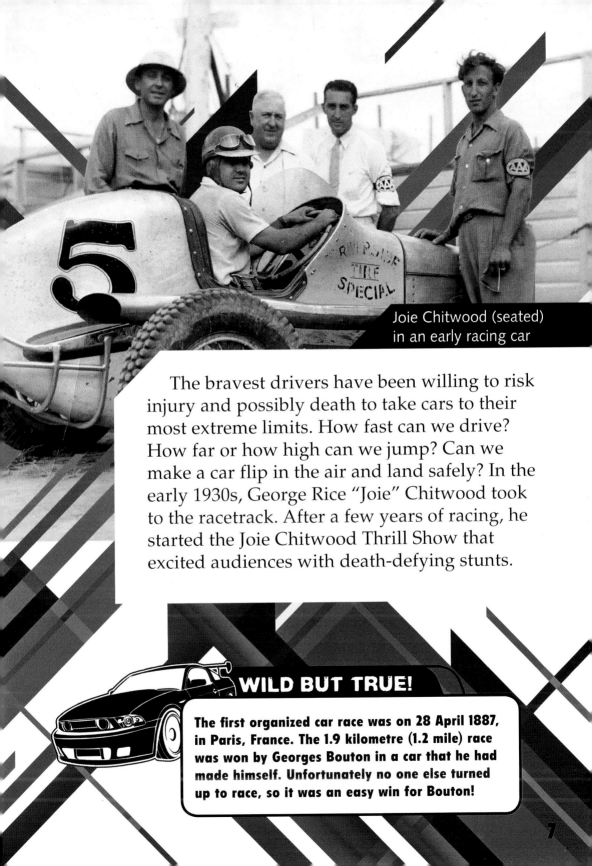

Joie Chitwood (seated) in an early racing car

The bravest drivers have been willing to risk injury and possibly death to take cars to their most extreme limits. How fast can we drive? How far or how high can we jump? Can we make a car flip in the air and land safely? In the early 1930s, George Rice "Joie" Chitwood took to the racetrack. After a few years of racing, he started the Joie Chitwood Thrill Show that excited audiences with death-defying stunts.

WILD BUT TRUE!

The first organized car race was on 28 April 1887, in Paris, France. The 1.9 kilometre (1.2 mile) race was won by Georges Bouton in a car that he had made himself. Unfortunately no one else turned up to race, so it was an easy win for Bouton!

Daredevils behind the wheel

The early 1900s was the era of silent films. Wallace Reid was a popular actor whose good looks and charm made him a favourite on the silver screen. When Reid wasn't acting, he was driving or working on cars. He brought his love of driving to the film world. He starred in *The Roaring Road* in 1919 and *Double Speed* and *Excuse My Dust* in 1920. These action-packed films showcased grand car chases and wild racing scenes.

"Whether speeding down an open road or through the air, I feel a surge of blood through my veins that prompts me to ever-increasing speeds."
Wallace Reid

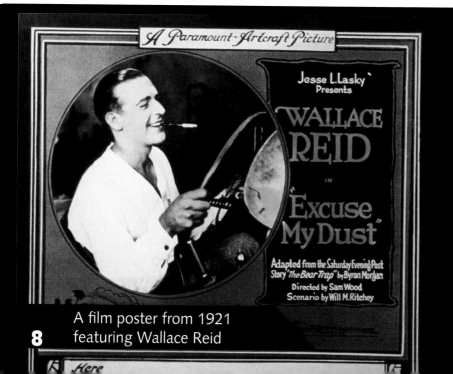

A film poster from 1921 featuring Wallace Reid

The Ford Model T was first made available in 1908. The earliest models had top speeds of 40-45 miles (64-72 km) per hour.

Pioneers such as Reid set the stage for other stuntmen to test the limits of cars. British driver Terry Grant was born in 1970 and began driving at the age of six. Driving around his family's farm, he discovered that he had talent. Grant now holds many Guinness World Records for stunt driving, including the fastest one-mile (1.6 kilometres) time for driving in reverse. In 2013 he set the record for circular "doughnut" spins, pulling off 39 doughnuts in 100 seconds.

pioneer person who is the first to try something new

Elements of the car stunt

The evolution of car stunts

There were only a few types of car in the early 1900s. As more and more models were created, the desire to compare them grew. What better way to compare two cars than to race them? Over time cars grew faster and more powerful. Naturally, drivers longed to see just what else these new machines could do.

Early cars were very heavy. They didn't go very fast. But drivers worked with what they had. They learned how to manoeuvre wheels in order to make cars do extraordinary things. Today's cars are lighter, faster and better *engineered* for stunt driving than ever before. That means that today's stunts are also bigger and better.

 CHECK THIS OUT! The first seat belt was invented by British engineer George Cayley in the late 1800s.

engineer make something happen using a scientific plan

An early car jumps over a "fallen bridge" in a promotional stunt from the 1920s

Ramping it up

Drivers need special equipment to push the limits of stunt driving. Some of the first stunts were jumps. To get cars *airborne*, cars need lift. To get lift, cars use ramps. Ramps come in a variety of sizes and shapes to help drivers create astonishing stunts. Some ramps are very large in order to help launch cars into long or very high jumps. Other ramps are small and help drivers get the car up on two wheels. For jumps that include spinning or flipping the car, ramps need to be specially designed using very precise *calculations*. With the right ramp and the right speed, drivers can pull off thrilling stunts.

Drivers need a place to perform their stunts. Special tracks that are in isolated environments help keep both the drivers and spectators safe. Stunts should never be attempted on public roads.

www.scottmaydaredevil

SCOTT MAY'S DAREDEV

DAF

airborne carried by the air; in flight

calculation use of a mathematical process to determine an outcome

WILD BUT TRUE!

The best-selling driving video game series is *Need for Speed*. From 1994 to 2014, the popular game sold nearly 100 million copies.

Alexei Latotsky performs
a flaming car stunt

Preparing for the worst

It is no secret that car stunts are dangerous. High speeds, crash landings and sudden stops are all a part of stunt driving. Rollovers, crashes and crash landings occur even when car stunts go according to plan. It's important that drivers protect themselves and follow safety precautions.

All stunt drivers wear protective helmets when doing stunts. Seatbelts that are specially made keep them strapped in even if their cars roll over. Their suits are made of special materials that protect them in case a fire breaks out.

The cars are also specially made with safety in mind. They have strong brakes so they can stop quickly. They also have extra strong *shock absorbers* to soften the impact of landing jumps. The frames of the cars are usually *reinforced*. This helps to maintain the car's shape in a crash and protect the driver inside.

CHECK THIS OUT! Stunt driver Hal Needham claims that he has broken as many as 56 bones in his body while performing stunts.

shock absorber device on a vehicle that lessens the impact of driving on rough surfaces, allowing a smoother ride

reinforce strengthen the structure or shape of something

Famous stunt men and stunt women

Carey Loftin began his stunt-driving career in the 1930s. He became known as a legendary Hollywood stunt man. By the 1960s he was sought after for the most challenging chase scenes and stunts. Loftin was a driver for *The Dukes of Hazzard*, a TV series that aired from 1979–1985 and was known for its chases and wild jumps. His chase scene in 1968's *Bullitt* with Steve McQueen is considered one of the best in film history.

When the director of 1984's *Against All Odds* needed a stunt man for a thrilling Ferrari chase scene, he turned to Loftin. Even though Loftin was 68 years old by that time, he was still considered the best in the business. Loftin was a stunt man who managed to avoid serious injury throughout most of his career. He worked as a stunt driver for more than 60 years with 195 stunt credits to his name.

WILD BUT TRUE!

Carey Loftin was asked to work on the set of the 1990 film *The Rookie* with Clint Eastwood. Well into his 70s by then, Loftin was asked mainly to share stories of his greatest stunts with the film's cast and crew.

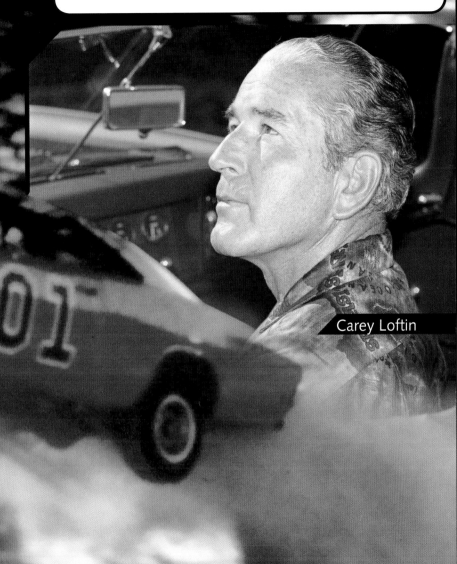

Carey Loftin

CHECK THIS OUT! *The Dukes of Hazzard* featured an orange Dodge Charger called The General Lee. *Dukes* stunt drivers wrote-off more than 300 General Lees in seven years.

With the right car and an ability to take calculated risks, modern stunt drivers are ready for anything.

Bill Hickman made a film career out of performing behind the wheel. Hickman's work in the 1971 film *The French Connection* is considered **legendary**. In that film, one memorable scene features a car wildly chasing an elevated train.

Scott Waugh watched his dad do stunts and grabbed the wheel for a 20-year career as a stunt man. In 2014, he directed the film *The Need for Speed*, which included many dramatic chase scenes.

Travis Pastrana is fearless. He drives in NASCAR races and holds the record for the longest jump by a rally car. He has also won several X Games medals and become equally famous for his **motocross** feats.

Experts plan a stunt for the 1973 film *The Seven*

"We went back out on the road, travelling at high speeds and hanging out the side of the car to film this. I wanted the audiences to really feel what it's like to drive 230 miles [370 km] per hour."

Scott Waugh, on filming *The Need for Speed*

A stunt scene from the 2014 film *The Need for Speed*

legendary remarkable enough to be well-known or famous

motocross cross-country motorbike race over an off-road circuit

19

Move over men – there are plenty of women who can take the wheel, too. From the beginning of automobile history, women have also been fascinated by cars.

In 1916, actress Gloria Swanson was hooked after her first driving lesson. She went on to star in films such as *The Danger Girl* and *Sunset Boulevard* that featured her in cars.

"I turned out to be a natural [driver]. I quickly learned to wheel around in tight circles, go into instant reverse, and take bumps and curves."
Gloria Swanson

Gloria Swanson

Georgia Durante's first appearances on TV were as a model. Durante learned how to drive early in life. She even briefly worked as a getaway driver for some members of the mob! She turned that into a career as a stunt driver in films, TV shows and advertisements, mainly in the 1990s.

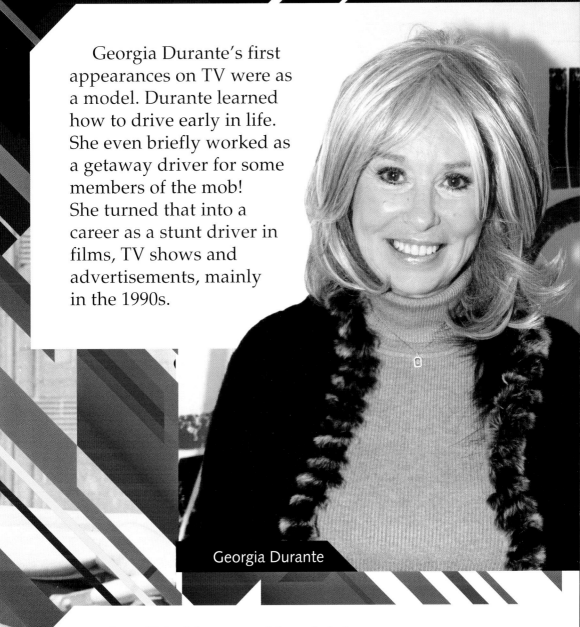

Georgia Durante

Sera Trimble started her driving career as a hotel valet in Seattle, USA. When a director saw her park a car while driving very fast, he nudged her into a career as a stunt driver. Trimble has driven in car advertisements as well as on the set of the TV series *Hawaii Five-O*.

The wildest car stunts

Some stunts have been done over and over again. Others are so daring and so imaginative that they never lose their wow factor.

The double loop track

Just like on a Hot Wheels toy track, Tanner Foust and Greg Tracy drove their life-size Hot Wheels cars through a fully-looped track. That means that at one point their cars were actually upside down. While this stunt did not require extreme speeds, there was a lot of danger involved.

Backflip

The backflip is a stunt that has been attempted many times unsuccessfully. But in 2013, French stunt driver Guerlain Chicherit pulled it off in spectacular fashion. Driving a modified Mini Countryman car, Chicherit sped off of a specially designed ramp. Then he completed a 360-degree backflip in mid-air before landing on a 7.9-metre (26-ft) high snow ramp. The snow softened the landing, giving this amazing stunt a perfect ending.

In 2013, Hot Wheels attempted a single-car, double-loop stunt with a *drone* car, but it crashed.

drone unmanned, remote-controlled vehicle

Stunts on the silver screen

James Bond films are known for their crazy stunts. For the 1974 film *The Man with the Golden Gun*, stunt driver Lauren "Bumps" Willert pulled off an amazing feat. Willert made the first ever filmed *barrel roll* jump by hitting a corkscrewed ramp and jumping over a river. This stunt was years ahead of its time and made for a fantastic film scene.

barrel roll type of inversion in which a vehicle turns in a circle sideways

CHECK THIS OUT!

The car used in the barrel roll stunt from *The Man with the Golden Gun* was a 1974 AMC Hornet X Hatchback.

In 2005's *Batman Begins*, stunt man George Cottle raced Batman's Tumbler vehicle through the streets of Gotham, which was actually Chicago, USA. Many versions of the Tumbler were created – one with a real jet engine fuelled by six propane tanks. The filmmakers wanted to film the action scenes with the Tumbler. They were looking for a realistic, rather than digital, effect. Cottle could not see out of the windscreen, so he had to rely on TV monitors inside the vehicle.

Jumping, sliding and spinning into the record books

As soon as someone has completed a stunt, someone else wants to do it better. These drivers aren't afraid to attempt the impossible.

Tanner Foust sets the distance jump on 29 May, 2011, in Indiana, USA.

Distance jump record

Tanner Foust is a rally car driver and X Games champion. He was the first car driver to do a full loop. He also holds the record for the longest jump by a four-wheeled vehicle of 101 metres (332 ft).

Tight parking spot

In November 2014, Chinese stunt driver Han Yue set the world *drift* parking record. Speeding towards a parking space that was just 8 centimetres (3.15 inches) longer than his Mini Cooper, Yue pulled the brake and slid the car sideways straight into the space.

drift controlled power slide that takes place around a curve

Longest distance on two wheels

In 2009, Italian driver Michele Pilia drove his specially modified BMW car on just two wheels for 371,07 kilometres (230.57 miles). By driving just one side of the car off of a small ramp, he was able to pop it up onto two wheels. Keeping the car balanced for so long required intense concentration and skill. The car's modifications redistributed the weight of the car to help it balance.

Guerlain Chicherit makes his world-record attempt on 18 March, 2014.

Longest car jump in reverse

In 2014, driver Rob Dyrdek launched his Chevrolet Sonic RS an amazing 27.21 metres (more than 89 feet) through the air while driving in reverse. He had to drive backwards very quickly, hit the ramp, and land safely on the opposite ramp to complete the record. He spun out on the landing and ran the car into a protective wall but was not hurt. Dyrdek performs reality TV stunts and is also a professional skateboarder.

CHECK THIS OUT! French driver Guerlain Chicherit attempted to break Tanner Foust's long distance jump record in 2014. Unfortunately, his 110-metre (360-ft) attempt ended in a fiery wreck. Luckily, Chicherit survived.

Glossary

airborne carried by the air; in flight

barrel roll type of inversion in which a vehicle turns in a circle sideways

calculation use of a mathematical process to determine an outcome

drift controlled power slide that takes place around a curve

drone unmanned, remote-controlled vehicle

engineer make something happen using a scientific plan

legendary remarkable enough to be well-known or famous

manoeuvre planned and controlled movement that requires skill

motocross cross-country motorbike race over an off-road circuit

pioneer person who is the first to try something new

reinforce strengthen the structure or shape of something

shock absorber device on a vehicle that lessens the impact of driving on rough surfaces, allowing a smoother ride

Read more

Cars (Design and Engineering), Ian Graham (Raintree, 2013)

Cars and Motorbikes (Science and Technology), John Townsend (Raintree, 2012)

Race that Bike! Forces in Vehicles (Feel the Force), Angela Royston (Raintree, 2015)

Super Cool Forces and Motion Activities (Max Axiom Science and Engineering), Agnieszka Biskup (Raintree, 2015)

Websites

www.beaulieu.co.uk
Uncover the history of the British Land Speed Record attempts, including photographs, fact cards and driver biographies at the famous Beaulieu Motor Museum's website.

www.guinnessworldrecords.com
Search the Guinness World Records website for astounding car stunts and records, including the smallest roadworthy car, the most participants in a car race and the fastest remote-controlled car!

Index